CHÍDÌNMA

God Is Good

GW01451657

Chidinma B. Naze

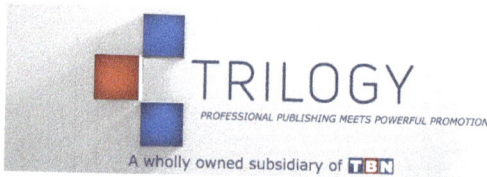

Trilogy Christian Publishers

A Wholly Owned Subsidiary of Trinity Broadcasting Network

2442 Michelle Drive Tustin, CA 92780

For information, address Trilogy Christian Publishing

Rights Department, 2442 Michelle Drive, Tustin, CA 92780.

10 9 8 7 6 5 4 3 2 1

Library of Congress Cataloging-in-Publication Data is available.

ISBN 979-8-89333-337-4 | ISBN 979-8-89333-338-1

Dedication

I want to say that this book is dedicated to God, but I feel strongly that this book is from God dedicated to everyone who reads it. I thank God for using me in this capacity to spread His love and kindness to the world. I am on this earth to serve Him and I couldn't think of a more honorable position. Thank You, God my Father, for everything! Thank You, Jesus Christ, my Lord and Savior, for teaching me the true meaning of love. Thank You, Holy Spirit, for being my friend, teacher, and guiding help.

To my son, Josephus Tobechukwu Jordan Jr., and my children to come: I love you so much, but I want you to know that as much as I love you, God, your Creator, your real Father, loves you even more. He loves you in a way you may never be able to fully comprehend. Of all the gifts I give you, this is the biggest of all. The knowledge that the Creator of heaven and earth and all in it loves you exceedingly and abundantly more than you could ever ask or imagine. No matter what goes on in your life, please never depart from Him. Seek Him first and everything else will follow. This I promise you. As you can read, and hopefully see, I am a living testimony of that truth. The thing is, even when we don't seek Him, He finds us and yanks us by the waist as a good father does. I pray He doesn't have to come looking for you like He did Adam in the Garden of Eden. I pray you knock on His door and He opens it, recognizing you immediately because your father and I will make sure you are dedicated to Him from birth. No matter what we do though, He knew your name before you were born because He made you.

No matter how many times you fall or sin, please never give up on Him because He never gives up on you. God knows you more than you know yourself, so never let the devil deceive you into believing your sin is ever too great to return to your God. The blood of Jesus and the grace of God are sufficient for you. I love you with my whole heart. May the good Lord bless you and shine His light on you now and forevermore.

To my darling husband, Josephus T. Jordan. Your support for me is one for the books. Oh wait, I am writing it in a book right now. You are my special gift from God and I love you so much.

To my father and mother, Fidelis and Benedicta Naze. My siblings, Ijeoma, Onyinye, Ekeneme, Uchechi, and Chinonso. My brothers-in-law and sister-in-law, Benard Nzerem, Onyekwere Ukoha, Sonny Filipovic, and Helen Naze.

DEDICATION

My nephews and nieces, Onyedikachi, Chimkadibia, Chigaemezu, Kenna, Ziora, and Luka. I love you so so so much and I thank you for all the love and support you have shown me. God bless you!

To my friends, I feel God's love through you every day. Thank you.

Contents

Foreword

I knew you before I formed you in your mother's womb. Before you were born I set you apart and appointed you as my prophet to the nations.

Jeremiah 1:5, NLT

I am often led to this verse when I think of my life's journey. I have come to realize that though it is termed "my life," it is not entirely my own. I am a vehicle filled with gifts, appointed to make many stops, sharing with others the gifts God has filled within me. I am one of the many souls put on earth to fulfill God's purpose. It is not just about me.

One of the first lessons God taught me is that *selfishness is not a gift of the Holy Spirit,* so here I am sharing many vital parts of my story as directed by God, to help someone through this journey called Life.

I hope this strengthens your faith, gives you hope, and shows you that miracles still happen.

The Genesis

It was around 5:00 p.m. on the third Monday in May 1992, May 18, to be exact. My mother, Chiatogu Benedicta Naze, eager to meet me, went into labor. All the mango cravings and indulgent satisfactions had paid off. I was coming. Her sixth and last child. She had this exact "last child" plan seven years ago when she had my older sister, Chinonso. As my existence shows, that plan didn't work, so here she was again. Another labor, another prayer.

In my mother's usual form, this was just another normal day going to the hospital to have a baby. After five children, she had mastered the art of childbearing. The *labor conqueror* might as well have been her middle name. The delivery ward, as I imagine, was her game room.

"Quick and easy as usual," she thought. But this time in the delivery room minutes turned to hours, hours to even more hours, and I was not even close to being born yet. One minute she was in labor and the next she wasn't. Her body became more and more exhausted each time.

The nurses, after sensing that something was wrong, called for the Matron, who was a senior nurse and also the wife of the owner of the hospital. The Matron walked in, checked on my mother, held her hands, and informed her that they were all going to take a break as it probably wasn't time for my birth yet. She spoke to my mother briefly and was about to leave when suddenly, she screamed in discomfort, "Madam, let go of my hand." My mother, who became confused, responded, "I don't understand. I am not holding onto your hand." They tried to release the grasp of each other's hands, to no avail.

Still very puzzled, the Matron took a huge sigh, sat next to my mother, and stared at their hands. After sitting for some minutes, she said to my mother, "Since I can't leave now, I might as well check on you and the baby again." In that moment, just like in the Bible story when Zechariah's tongue was freed after he wrote "his name is John," the Matron and my mother's hands were freed.

They couldn't believe what had happened. They couldn't make any sense of it, but the Matron proceeded to check on my mother and me. As she began to carry out the medical check, she screamed out to the nurses, "Pass me the scissors!"

She noticed that the umbilical cord had been wrapped all around me, stopping me from moving and weakening my mother and me during labor.

My mother says that once the Matron cut the cords off me, I popped out with some cords still wrapped around my neck and feet. The cords had been obstructing my breathing and made it difficult for her to push during labor. Some minutes after I was born, my breathing returned to normal and my mother and I started to feel better.

While all this was going on, there was no light. The city of Port Harcourt, Nigeria, had a week-long power outage, so I was born in a room lit up by a candle.

> Neither do men light a candle, and put it under a bushel, but on a candlestick; and it giveth light unto all that are in the house. In the same way, let your light shine before men, that they may see your good works, and glorify your Father in heaven."

Matthew 15–6, KJV

My father, my mother and I

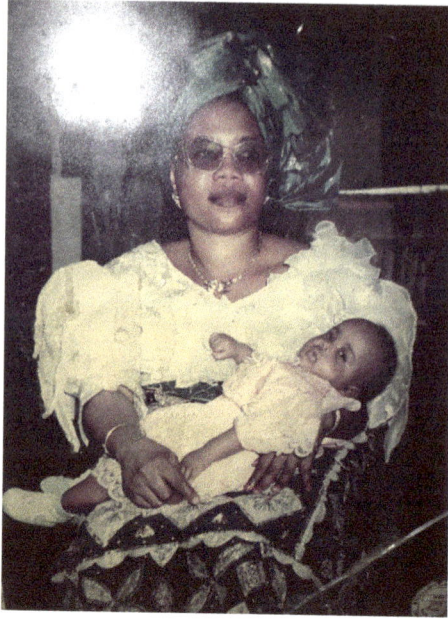

My mother and I

That was the first of many miracles God performed in my life. The genesis of the many times God showed up and saved me.

Chapter 1

GOD, MY FATHER

Growing up as the "baby of the house" as I'm fondly called by my family, my father never spared an expense for my birthdays. If I wanted it, I got it. If I didn't think of it, I still got it. This was also the case for my tenth birthday, which I often refer to as the highlight of my childhood.

Every child has certain moments that inform their lives and build their self-esteem. For me, there are two I remember vividly: my tenth birthday party and Maltina.

Maltina is a malt drink found in Nigeria. When I was younger, children who drank this were seen as too forward, too bold, and often times, greedy or eager to become adults before their time. This was because Maltina was more expensive than the other soda drinks and it was mostly drunk by older women.

Of course, little Chidinma loved nothing else but this drink. While other children oohed and aahed for sweet sodas, I woahed for Maltina. At birthday parties I would see other parents tell their children not to drink Maltina because it was for "adults," but my mother would loudly and proudly encourage me to speak up about my preference when asked what I would drink. Even with her support, I would timidly respond, "I want Maltina, please." I still remember rooms of people going judgmentally silent on many occasions after my order, but my mother, holding her head and shoulders high, would strongly reiterate, "My daughter said she wants Maltina."

Growing up, I've found myself mimicking that same stance while standing up for myself and others. With that one drink of Maltina, my mother taught me to be myself boldly.

As I mentioned earlier, my tenth birthday party was a big deal to me. Thinking back, I don't know where I got the idea that ten was a monumental number. I just knew that I was turning ten and it meant something, so my party had to be BIG. At the time, there was no venue bigger than Delight Zone in Port Harcourt. It was a small but mighty amusement park like no other. The rides, the food, the pure joy in the atmosphere, and the *price!*

Nine-year-old Chidinma didn't care about that price. She had the confidence that her father would give her anything her heart desired as long as it was good. Her father was Superman in her eyes, so nothing could limit him and she was right. As soon as I mentioned my elaborate birthday plans of renting out Delight Zone to my father, he responded, "Anything you want, Chidinma."

It wasn't just my father who was on board, my sweet sister Onyinye, who was very pregnant at the time, stopped everything she had going on and became my party planner. We went shopping for custom made birthday cards, souvenirs for guests, and of course, a Barbie birthday cake to fit the occasion.

On the day of my party, I dressed up in a white ball gown like a bride on her wedding day. My hair was braided up in a bun with two strategically placed single braids falling from each side to frame my face. I called it the "Alicia Keys," an ode to her early hairstyles, but to my Nigerian mother and her little knowledge of pop culture, it quickly became the "Alika She."

Me at my 10th birthday party

That day, everyone from my family, to family friends, uncles and aunties, friends and loved ones, rallied together, showed up, and showed out for me. Their undiluted love made me feel like a princess. It taught me at a young age the value of service to others, not just to one's self. The party was spectacular! It was everything I could have imagined and more.

Sitting in my room at the end of the day, the wheels in my mind started to turn. "If my earthly father could do all this for me, then surely my heavenly Father could do more!" As quickly as that thought came, another one followed: "Why don't I ever ask God for a birthday present?"

The same way I was so confident that my father could give me anything my heart desired because it was good, I was, and still am, convinced that God, who created my father and gave my father the task to watch over me on earth, could do even more.

This thought wasn't a selfish one. It wasn't about a little child finding ways to get more things. It was about understanding the true Source of power and surrendering my existence to Him.

This birthed a new tradition for me. Every year since, I ask God for a birthday present. Sometimes I pray for things I need and sometimes I ask Him to give me what He pleases. Every year I ask, and every year I get. He has not failed me once!

It is important for me to elucidate that in my requests, I still surrender. I first say, "God, may Your will be done." If it does not align with His will for me, I don't want it. God sees and knows things we might never see and know.

With God by my side, I have learned to not be anxious. Besides, *anxiety is not a gift of the Holy Spirit.*

> Do not be anxious about anything, but in every situation, by prayer and petition, with thanksgiving, present your requests to God. And the peace of God, which transcends all understanding, will guard your hearts and your minds in Christ Jesus.
>
> **Philippians 4:6–7**

My tenth birthday birthed a yearly birthday request; my yearly birthday requests birthed miracles.

Chapter 2

GOD, MY PROVIDER

In January 2016, I returned to Nigeria from the United States of America. I was in America for college at the University of Indianapolis, where I studied communication with an emphasis in electronic media. After college, I worked at CBS News and the Burmese American Community Institute in Indianapolis.

Growing up, I wanted to be a newscaster and TV presenter like Oprah, but I realized that being a newscaster in the forefront of so much sad news depressed me. The one thing I was sure of was that I wanted to live and work in Nigeria. I felt my love for my country strongly, and I knew that God had put that in my heart, so I let Him lead.

Nigeria has a vibe that can never be replicated anywhere else. It is rich in culture, food, and even with all the adversity my people have faced, it is rich in love and high in humor. I do not know a funnier set of people.

I returned to Nigeria against all advice from my family and friends. Some thought I was going crazy. They thought

I had tasted milk and honey in the promised land and I was about to trade it all for gall. I have never been one to listen to people at the expense of muting my own voice or the voice of Christ leading me, so I put my blinders on and headed home.

I was immensely excited. Upon my arrival, my parents put up a banner in our home that said, "Welcome Home, Bene!" which is the short form of my middle name, Benedicta, meaning blessed.

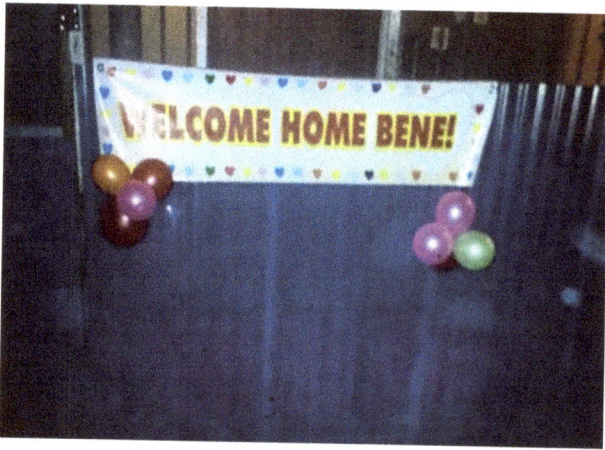

This homemade girl was on her home soil eating homemade egusi soup and pounded yam. Nobody could tell me anything. It was everything I spent years dreaming about.

All that was until the reality of NYSC yanked me out of my dreamland.

In Nigeria, every university graduate has to complete a National Youth Service Corps (NYSC) program before being allowed to work. The NYSC program was set up by the Nigerian government during the military regime to involve Nigerian graduates in nation building and the development of the country. Graduates of universities and polytechnics are required to take part in this NYSC program for one year. This is known as the national service year.

A person serving in this NYSC program could be posted to any of the thirty-six states in Nigeria for the year. It is usually a different state from where one lives. It doesn't matter if it is a state you have never visited. If you get posted there, you serve there. First, you attend a three-week training boot camp, then you work for the government, usually as a teacher, until the year ends.

I was ready to register for my NYSC before finding a job, but the realization that I could be posted to any state put me in a mode of panic. I had planned to move specifically to Lagos, Nigeria for the good media opportunities there, so the possibility of being sent to somewhere I had never been, which could have been the middle of nowhere, was not in my plan. I understood the positive aspects of the initiative, but I had heard of Youth Corpers who had terrible experiences.

The government was firmly against any special treatment, as they should be. They didn't care if you were an international student, like they did previously, or who you knew. Anyone could be posted anywhere.

In the year I returned, the National Youth Service Corp resumption was delayed, so my batch was called to sign on just a few months before the month of May, my birthday. As you can guess, I knew exactly what I wanted to ask God to gift me for my birthday that year.

I wanted to be posted to Lagos and I wanted to work in a media company. As much as I loved children and wouldn't have minded teaching, I wanted to use the year to learn, network, and grow in the media space in Nigeria. I prayed and prayed over again to God about it.

As the time for the distribution of the digital posting letters came closer, my worry grew. In meditating on the Word of God, I was reminded that *fear is not a gift of the Holy Spirit.*

My dad was as worried as I was, or maybe even more. Whenever he would try to talk to me about his concerns, I would muster up courage and say, "Don't worry, Daddy, God is going to help me get posted to Lagos as my birthday present." He too is a firm believer in God, but I saw the look on his face that said, *I hope this girl doesn't get disappointed if this doesn't happen.*

"You had a good life in America, but you insisted on moving back here," he said, followed by a deep sigh of worry.

"Don't worry, Daddy, God is going to help me get posted to Lagos as my birthday present," I repeated.

The countdown gave us a lot of sleepless nights, and sometimes I wished the days moved slower, but time truly waits for no one.

The day of the posting announcements finally came. "Chidinma! Chidinma!" I heard my father calling outside my bedroom window. "The posting letters have been sent. Hurry, check where you've been posted." My heart started to beat so fast, like it was jumping out of my chest. I must have paced around my room for about twenty minutes before I finally decided to just check it.

I picked up my laptop and logged into the NYSC portal. With palms sweating and heart still beating, I clicked on the tab that said "PPA Letter." The first thing I saw when my letter opened up was "Imo State." My heart sunk. "They posted me to Imo State?" I said out loud. As I looked closely with tears welling up in my eyes, there was an ounce of hope because at least I knew people there. Then I realized that what I had just read was my state of origin. I burst out in loud laughter. Oh, the things fear could do. I kept reading, and that was when I saw it written inconspicuously, "State of Deployment: Lagos State."

I screamed with so much joy. I couldn't keep myself from jumping around my room. "God has done it! Daddy, Mummy, God has done it!" I ran down the stairs to my father and mother. "I've been posted to Lagos!" I screamed. My parents were so thrilled. They could not believe it. I told everyone I saw about my testimony. I was filled with so much gratitude. My future in Nigeria was finally shaping up.

In the usual human form, my joy was short-lived. I started to worry about something else. Now that I had gotten posted to the city I wanted, I wondered about the job I would be asked to do after the NYSC camp. Right after telling God that I had one major request, I went back into prayer mode and started asking for something else.

In my journey with God, I've realized that He is not man. Yes, we are made in His image, but He is supreme. He knows our needs before we know them. Sometimes, the Holy Spirit sees the groanings of our hearts and goes ahead to intercede on our behalf before we even speak a word. God always finishes what He starts and never leaves us halfway.

Unknown to me, in all my worry, God had already set a plan in motion. As things played out, I realized that God's plan had been playing out for a very long time in my life. Like building blocks forming a big house.

After university I wasn't one of the people who graduated with a job offer in their inboxes. I had a long waiting period where I was applying for jobs and almost getting them but never quite getting through. It was one heartbreak after the next.

In my life there have been many moments filled with thorns, but the spirit of gratitude has always kept me going. Gratitude reminds me that if I am still alive, then there's still hope. It reminds me that even if God never did anything else for me, the fact that He sent His only Son Jesus Christ to shed His blood for me that one time is enough for me to always be thankful. When things don't go as planned in my life, I think of all that has gone even better. Family, true friends, support systems, love, peace, oxygen, good health, the ability to move, see, eat, and the list goes on. Where your mind sets is where you become. If your mind is set on sadness, you become sad. If your mind is set on anger or bitterness, you become angry or bitter.

My Igbo people say, "Eto dike na nke omere, ome ozo," meaning if you praise a king/warrior/man of great strength for what he has done, he will do more. Gratitude leads to praise, and praise is like a first-class ticket to God. It ensures priority boarding because God loves our songs and beautiful gestures of praise. It gives us the best seats through the ride of life, and unlike worldly first-class tickets, it is free!

Refer to the "Gratitude Check" at the end of the book.

In that period of looking for employment, I had limited time to find one because of my international student status. I was advised to volunteer for a job in social media at the Burmese American Community Institute, a place I had volunteered at many times while in college. It wasn't the news job I wanted, and back then social media wasn't considered a serious job with moneymaking opportunities, but I went for it.

When I started the job I felt lost, but in no time I realized I was very good at it. I started to enjoy it and enjoy the ways my brain thought of media strategies. It was like unlocking another level of creativity.

Not too long after, I became their Head Social Media Manager. I still didn't know how I landed that position, but

I knew it felt good. My heart was at peace, which is usually my checker. If my heart isn't at peace, I don't do it, and if I have started it before the lack of peace kicks in, I don't continue it.

When I felt my beautiful time there had come to an end, I went on to work for CBS News. Time went by, and I still didn't know or fully understand why I was put in the position to have that social media job. Yes, I enjoyed it, but I didn't see the place it fit into the puzzle of my life...yet.

A week before NYSC camp was set to begin, I was lying down in bed feeling sad and scrolling through Instagram when I saw a flyer from a media company I followed online. The flyer stated that they were looking for a Social Media Intern in Lagos, Nigeria. I sat up quickly, read about the details in depth, and I knew that was it. I couldn't explain the feeling, but I knew that was the job I was meant to have for my NYSC and my next phase.

I sent my resume to the email in the flyer and I got a response shortly after asking me to come for an interview in three days. "Three days!" I wondered how I was going to get everything ready for NYSC camp and get on a flight to Lagos earlier than planned in three days. I decided not to tell my parents I was going for an interview so they wouldn't be worried or sad if I didn't get the job. I told them I had to go earlier than planned to prepare for NYSC camp. Thankfully, they agreed without asking too many questions. I got my flight tickets, packed my bags, and off Jesus and I went.

My flight was delayed, so I showed up to the interview a little late. I had sent them an email prior to the meeting, informing them of my situation and, thankfully, they understood. As I walked into the office, I saw some people all within my age range waiting in line for the interview as well. I looked around and envisioned myself working there. I took in deep breaths, tried to shun all feelings of nervousness, and waited my turn.

When it was my turn, a young middle-aged man called me up from the waiting area into a room that looked like a studio. There were huge lights, green screen backdrops, and props placed in different corners. Seated right in the middle of the room were three interviewers—two ladies and one man. It felt like I was about to audition for a big movie role, but in this case, the movie was my life.

I was starring in a movie about my life in that moment. Actually, in every moment. Isn't that what we do? Our whole lives are like one big movie that we only see in bits day by day, never knowing how it will end. Hoping for the best, but sometimes expecting the worst. We think we are the directors until we realize that someone other than ourselves has the ability to say "cut."

Once we know better, we try not to worry about the next day's scene because it is not promised. We try to live in the moment, take nothing for granted, love deeply, forgive deeply, create healthy boundaries, and show kindness to all. The wise ones seek the kingdom of God first and know that everything else will follow.

I walked up to the interviewers, introduced myself, and the interview began. "We saw you worked as a social media manager before you worked at CBS. That got our attention," they said as I tried to hide a smile. What an irony life is sometimes. The things we begrudgingly accept could sometimes be the things that help us.

A few questions later, they made a hypothetical offer. "If we were to offer you this position, we would like you to start right away. Is that a problem?" My eyes widened like I had just seen my NEPA bill (electric bill).

"I'm going to NYSC camp in a few days," I blurted out. "I was hoping to start in a few weeks right after camp."

Their smile turned upside down as they responded, "Sadly, we don't hire Youth Corpers, but we'll give you a call on our decision. It was really nice to meet you." I mustered up a polite smile, thanked them for their time, and walked out of the studio and… "Scene!"

I was hoping a director would pop out of somewhere, shout that, and say, "Take two!" In the movie of our lives, even though we are not the directors, as I mentioned earlier, we are not powerless. We have free will. We are expected to do our best and make the best decisions so that our stories have a better chance of a happy ending.

After the interview, I proceeded to pick up my suitcase that I had left at the security man's office when I heard him say, "How the interview go? No worry, Madam, you don get am already," he said in pidgin English, reassuring me with a smile that I had gotten the job.

I smiled in return and agreed, "Yes, oh, I don get am." In that moment, I said to myself, "Positive affirmations, Chidinma. If you give up in your mind, then you have given up in real life and you are not a quitter."

I sensed that man was there to pick me up when I felt down. Sometimes we expect God to come out of the clouds to solve our problems while disregarding the fact that we are surrounded by people who are made in the image of God. God uses these people to show up for us. It doesn't matter the societal positions they occupy or the way they look. They have God in them. We are all answers to each other's prayers. That is one of the reasons it is important that we are intentional in doing our part—for ourselves and for others.

With the little fuel pumped into me by the security man's quick talk, I decided to use my free will to send an email to the interviewers thanking them again for their time, highlighting the skills I would be bringing to the company if I were hired, and expressing my eagerness to hear from them soon. I also expressed that I was willing to do any work needed of me while at NYSC camp. As Marvin Gaye said, "Ain't no mountain high enough."

I ordered an Uber and headed to a friend's place. Lagos traffic welcomed me with open arms. The ride was long, but I was thankful. I was finally going to be a resident of the city I used to read about in Genevieve magazines. The city my dad used to take me to when he traveled for work so I could see the ships at the seaports in Apapa and have Sunday brunches with him at the famous EKO Hotel. The city felt familiar but had many new prospects.

As I was delving deeper into my thoughts, my phone rang. It was a number I didn't have saved, but I picked up because as the Igbo girl in me always says, "You never know when money will call."

"Hello Chidinma, this is Monica from Ebonylife TV." My heart started beating so fast that it could have made beats for the dance groups in my village. I quickly composed myself.

"Hello Monica, nice to hear from you." I wasn't sure if I had lied or told the truth.

"I am pleased to inform you that you have been offered the Social Media Internship position. We usually don't employ Corpers, but we decided to make an exception in your case."

Remember when I said God uses people to show up for us? Apparently Monica, who was one of the interviewers, had spoken up and made a good case for me. Someone whom I had never met before the interview sent emails and made calls to convince the people at the top to give me a chance. God had blessed me with favor and let the light He put in me shine through. I didn't know what else to say other than, "Thank you. I am highly appreciative of this opportunity and look forward to joining the team."

After the phone call, I was beaming with joy. I called my family to inform them about the good news. God had sorted me out once again. It felt like I was an immigrant and in one day, Lagos city had given me a permanent residency.

Thinking back, that moment was one of "opportunity meeting preparation." If I had not been put in a position where I had to go through disappointments and then be forced to do my first social media job, I would not have been prepared for this social media job. If I had not passed the previous life test, I might not have been able to graduate and get an admission into this next class of life. As my mother always says, "Every disappointment is a blessing." In that moment, it all came full circle.

> In their hearts humans plan their course, but
> the LORD establishes their steps.

Proverbs 16:9

To me, this story was over. This scene had come to a great end. God had done His part and now it was my turn to take the torch and run the rest of the race. All was well.

Some days after the interview, I packed my things and headed to the NYSC camp grounds. I didn't really know what to expect, but I was determined to blend in with the crowd. I had been in the United States for a significant amount of time, but my core was still 100 percent Nigerian. It ran so deep in my blood that I basically bled green, white, green.

Upon my arrival at camp, I noticed that it was filled

with vibrant people from different tribal, economic, and educational backgrounds. A true melting pot. It felt like the positive aspects of boarding school all over again. I was having a lovely time until I heard, "No one here will be posted to any job they think they already have. The only job you will render your NYSC service to is the one we choose and assign to you," the camp director yelled out at our first camp meeting.

"Here we go again!" I thought. Just when I thought one problem was handled, another reared its unpleasant head. That was it. All the hard work I did was for nothing. I was going to spend my one year of NYSC learning nothing about my actual career path.

At this point I had maximized my level of worry that my cup had runneth over and had no more space to hold any more emotions. I became numb. "God, I'm tired," I mumbled under my breath.

Thankfully, when we are tired, God has strength. Even in our sin and unworthiness, God's plan for us is to be happy and prosperous. He is always there waiting with open arms, ready to take care of us.

> For I know the plans I have for you,' declares
> the Lord, 'plans to prosper you and not to harm
> you, plans to give you a hope and a future.

Jeremiah 29:11

A few days later, I was walking with some friends to the mammy market to get some food when I heard, "Hey you!" I turned around calmly. It was a man dressed in an army uniform leaning on a car. As I began to walk towards him, he said, "I want sunglasses. Will you buy me sunglasses?"

I was confused at such an odd request. I thought, "Out of everyone here, why me?" This man didn't know me and he was asking me to buy him some sunglasses. "Okay. Do you have any one in particular you want?" I casually responded.

"You'll do it? Ah, thank you. Just buy any one you think will fit me," he said. Thankfully, I always walked around camp with some money in my pouch, so I went into the mammy market, bought him a thoroughly picked pair of sunglasses, and handed it over to him.

Once he saw the glasses, he beamed with gratitude. He was pleased with the choice I had made for him. "Is there an office you want to be posted to? What is your name and registration number? Write all your information down and give it to me. I will help you." The words he uttered sounded like the most beautiful song I had ever heard. What was this man saying to me? I feigned a small level of incoherence just to get him to repeat himself and he repeated the exact words. With the speed of light, I pulled out a piece of paper and a pen from my pouch, wrote my information, and gave it to him. Two weeks later, I was assigned to Ebonylife TV as my official place of work. No, this was not a bribe; it was grace and favor. God works in mysterious ways.

I have grown to realize that fear can be a sin. Whenever we give in to fear, we disobey God. Many times in the Bible God said, "Do not be afraid." I used to think it was only advice, but I have come to learn that it is also an order. It is a teaching and a direction on what not to do.

The spirit of fear does what the devil does: kills, steals, and destroys. It is a tool used by the devil and it tries to restrict us from moving forward. I no longer believe in the saying, "Do it afraid." Instead, I say, "Do it boldly!" as the child of the King of Kings and Lion of the tribe of Judah. Do it boldly as the one who is said to inherit the kingdom and even to judge angels. God has not given us the spirit of fear, but according to 2 Timothy 1:7, He has given us the spirit of power, love and a sound mind/self-control.

Whenever I feel fear trying to creep in now, I do what I learnt from Prophetess Tiphani Montgomery. I repent of my sins or anything that could have opened the door to fear. I renounce and rebuke the spirit of fear and all spirits that are not the spirit of God, and I repair my mind, body, spirit, soul, and environment by inviting the Holy Spirit in to every situation. I also plead the blood of Jesus Christ over everything. The blood of Jesus frees us from sin (Revelation 1:5), forgives our trespasses (Ephesians 1:7), justifies and saves us (Romans 5:9).

The Holy Spirit also taught me to pray 2 Corinthians 10:5: "Casting down imaginations, and every high thing that exalteth itself against the knowledge of God, and bringing into captivity every thought to the obedience of Christ" (KJV).

Instead of doing things afraid, now I remember that "I can do all things through Christ who strengthens me" (Philippians 4:13, NKJV).

God always takes care of His own.

Me at NYSC camp

I have told the story of my NYSC journey, but something many people don't know is that there was a time I couldn't see myself having a journey at all.

Chapter 3

GOD, MY LIFELINE

For college, I had been accepted into the university of my choosing. At my sister's graduation ceremony in 2001, one of her professors took a look at me and said, "Which university would you like to go to when you grow up?"

My eight-year-old vivacious self looked around and responded, "This one. The University of Indianapolis." Ten years later, I got an admission to enroll in a four-year course to study communication with an emphasis in electronic media at the University of Indianapolis.

My mother, me, my sister Ijeoma

College started out as a beautiful and exciting experience, but quickly turned into a world of culture shock, with roommates who made fun of me for chewing on my bone after eating chicken (this definitely makes me chuckle now), and people who asked me if I grew up with lions in my home in "Africa."

"Africa" is not a country.

I thought I was ready for independence because I had attended a boarding high school, but I had no idea what the feeling of being on my own entailed. Coming from Nigeria, I was used to community. Everyone helping each other in different areas of difficulty and everyone being in everyone's business. As intrusive as that could feel sometimes, it creates a sense of family wherever you go.

In the U.S, I found out quickly that the latter wasn't the case. It was every man/woman to himself/herself. People were kind, but kind with many boundaries. Everyone worked hard for their money, so "money back" was usually their first agenda. For example, public transportation wasn't the best in Indianapolis at the time, so some of my fellow students had cars—but I didn't. This made me depend on people for car rides to get to places. I noticed that when I would ask someone to give me a ride to go to the same location they were going, they would ask me to pay them for the gas to get there. The same would happen if we had class trips or needed to pick up school supplies off campus. I understood we were all struggling students, but asking for gas money to the same location they were going to threw me off.

I was almost finally getting the hang of it when the biggest culture shock to create a dent in my pocket occurred. I was invited to a friend's birthday party at a steak house in downtown Indianapolis. I was really excited because, let's just say, the only thing I love more than food is God. At the dinner, I ordered an appetizer and an entrée, and assumed the birthday cake would be the dessert. I remember thoroughly enjoying the succulent and well-seasoned lamb chops and mashed potatoes when I noticed the waiter passing out each person's bill. "I must be confused," I thought. "Surely no one invites people for a birthday party and expects the people to pay for their own food."

In Nigeria, this is a major faux pa. In fact, it would never happen. Well, it was happening and my college student bank account and I never forgot it. Again, every man/woman for himself/herself—even at birthday celebrations. The con of those moments was that the culture shocked me and my bank account. The pro was, it taught me never to feel entitled to anyone's time and resources.

Other than these shocks, I realized that I was finding it difficult to become an "adult." I learned that my sense of identity was tied to the security my family's presence had provided me with for many years. Once I was alone, I became lost. Lost to myself and lost to the people who knew me. I became a shadow of myself. The spark in my eyes that I had grown up with turned dull.

I remember one of my brothers-in-law asking me if I was depressed. I had never even thought of the word or really knew what it meant, so I quickly answered, "No, I'm okay. I'm not depressed." Looking back now, I was definitely depressed. I stopped attending classes, couldn't read, stopped taking my family's calls, and would stay in my room with the lights turned off for long hours at a time without eating. I was doing all this while putting up a happy face in front of my college friends.

Only one friend noticed or at least said something. My dear Daniel, rest his soul. He was always checking on me, cooking for me, trying to get through to the issue he had perceived, but to no avail. I was a wall. Many people in my family were upset at my behavior, but they didn't realize that I was a wall to myself as well. No emotions were really coming through or making sense to me. Everything was dark. The lights were out.

With all the classes I had missed, I began to fail. I was inevitably put on academic probation for a semester. Once I found this out, the darkness grew darker. My parents were disappointed and decided to use the time I was out of school to bring me back to Nigeria. A part of me felt joy at the idea of returning home, but a bigger part of me became afraid of seeing and hearing my parents' disappointed looks and remarks in person.

In an African household, sometimes parents and elders think of how your life actions affect them before they think of how it affects you. They forget that no one can be in pain more than the person going through the issue. This stems from them sacrificing so much to give their children the best lives and education, but it can feel very harsh.

About two weeks before my flight to Nigeria, I went down on my knees, looked up to heaven, and prayed for God to take my life. I wanted to die. I specifically prayed for the flight to crash on my way to Nigeria. I was so lost in my mind that I never stopped to think of the other passengers on the flight. I just didn't want to be alive anymore. I looked at all the sharp objects around me and I knew I couldn't bring myself to end it all in one move, so I prayed. I wanted it painless and fast.

As the days until my flight got closer, I decided to write a note to myself as I usually did when I could not express myself properly. In the middle of the note, I wrote, "I wish I would die." Then suddenly, as if something else was writing for me, I wrote, "but I know it's going to be fine one day. This won't last forever."

As the days went by, I started to feel hope and strength beyond my understanding. It wasn't just in my writing; it was now in my head. Every time I would start to worry, the voice in my head would say, "It's going to be all right someday. You'll come out of this phase."

> My grace is sufficient for thee: for my strength
> is made perfect in weakness.

2 Corinthians 12:9, KJV

I made it to Nigeria in one piece. The plane crash was one prayer God did not answer. He gives us the desires of our heart *according to His will.*

The devil is a liar and the false promise of liberation through suicide is a lie of the enemy. He knows he will always lose to God, so he tries to cause the damnation of many souls before Jesus comes again. He knows that once someone dies, they no longer stand a chance to fight. That is why we need to put on the full armor of God and fight the devil in the name of Jesus.

God has given us authority to trample over snakes and scorpions and to overcome the power of the enemy (Luke 10:19) and has given Jesus the name above every other name that at the name of Jesus, every knee shall bow and every tongue shall confess that Jesus Christ is Lord! (Philippians 2:10–11)

Nigeria was the home I remembered. I felt grounded in a way I've come to realize I only feel in Nigeria. I was still ashamed to face my parents, so the casual "welcome back" greetings I got from them were more than enough for me. In fact, I wished those were the only words they would say to me during my stay, but those kinds of wishes don't come to pass in an African household.

Sooner than later, the questions ensued. "What has been going on with you?.... Why were you failing your classes?.... Why were you not taking our calls?.... Are you on drugs?"

My responses followed. "No, I'm not on drugs.... I don't know what's going on with me.... I think I'm better now." Then a very long silence. This quickly became a daily routine throughout my stay. At the end of most days, I would cry myself to sleep. I was miserable. It was undoubtedly the worst time of my life.

My former close relationship with my father became non-existent and my mother always looked at me with confusion in her eyes. My sister Onyinye, who was my only sibling in Nigeria at the time, the same sister who helped me with my tenth birthday party, became my main source of comfort. She never saw me the way everyone else saw me. She is usually the very vocal one, but she hardly ever brought up the conversation about my issues. Instead, she took me out for pedicures and movie dates whenever she could. Whenever I was next to her, I could feel God giving me a hug, and when I was alone, I could hear Him telling me to focus on the better future He had for me, even if I couldn't see it at the time.

I didn't know what was going to happen to me in regards to school, but I wanted another chance to finish my education in Indianapolis. I wrote a letter to the University of Indianapolis pleading my case and promising to do better if I was reinstated. I meant every word. I felt a preparedness I had not felt the first time I went. Hitting rock bottom left me looking into myself. My flaws, my weaknesses, my strengths, and more were all laid bare on the ground. There wasn't any fantasy land for me to live in anymore; only the gritty feeling of the rocks I lay bare on.

The only way left to go was up, and that was where I was determined to head towards.

Some weeks after I wrote the letter, I heard back from the university. I was reinstated. I shut off all the noise and put my blinders on. For the first time in my life, I wasn't living or failing for anyone else but myself.

I could see the fear in my parents' eyes as they kept asking me if I was sure I was ready to return to school. "Yes, I am," I quickly answered.

The old me would have fed off that fear, but the new me realized I had lost enough time to fear and sadness. I didn't want to die anymore. I was ready to live. With the help of God and my parents, I went back to Indianapolis to continue my education.

In all this, my parents still did not know half of what I was struggling with internally. They never knew I prayed for my life to be taken away. I'm sure they were almost as confused as I was at the time. They were hurt and they just wanted their bright shining baby girl to return as they remembered her to be. No one had given them a parental manual on this part of life, so it was a difficult time for them. Sadly, it was an even more difficult time for me, so I couldn't help them. I mean, I couldn't even help myself.

I returned to school a different person. It was as if I was put in a time capsule and I suddenly grew up emotionally, physically, mentally, and spiritually. At the end of my first semester back, I made the honor roll for "superior academic achievement." The next semester, I made the dean's list. God was taking me through and fulfilling on His promise for a better future.

If I had any doubt that God was helping me previously, this next story cleansed me of it all.

Chapter 4

GOD OF HOSTS

As a communication major, I had to take a class called Human Communication. It was one of my favorite classes taught by one of my favorite professors, Ms. Cunningham.

One day after class, Ms. Cunningham reminded us of our final class essay and gave us an assignment to make a list of the sources we were citing for the essay. In addition to the source list, we were to attach a paragraph from each source's findings regarding our individual topics. According to my understanding of her instructions, this was a very easy copy and paste assignment. All I had to do was copy the source's words and paste so Ms. Cunningham could have an idea on the direction of my essay.

The day to submit the assignment came, and it was like any other day. I woke up, got ready for the day, walked to the printing room, printed my assignment, and headed to class. I was sitting in class ready to turn in my work when I heard some of my classmates talking about the processes they used to paraphrase and summarize the words of their cited authors properly. *Paraphrase? Summarize?* I did no such thing. "These particular classmates could have misunderstood Ms. Cunningham," I thought. I went around asking my other classmates how they did the assignment and I realized that everyone had understood the memo but me. My stomach sank.

I had heard about plagiarism and the no tolerance policy the university had for it many times. In fact, anyone caught plagiarizing, knowingly or unknowingly, could automatically fail the course or be expelled from school.

My body was shaking. There was no time to redo the assignment, and I couldn't give the old excuse of "the dog ate it." To my dismay, I had no choice but to turn in my assignment to Ms. Cunningham. After class, I ran to my dorm room, knelt down, and prayed with so much fear and pain in my heart. I couldn't have survived so far just to end up failing the class or, worse, to be expelled. I didn't know what was going to happen or how it was going to happen, but I knew something extraordinary had to happen to get me out of this situation.

Ms. Cunningham's class took place twice every week, so for the next two days after the submission, I didn't eat or talk much. My stomach was in a constant knot. I worried, prayed, worried, and prayed again.

The day had come to receive our graded assignments back. I was sitting in class preparing myself to be called out or whatever procedure students had to go through before being expelled. Ms. Cunningham began sharing the papers from the back row. I usually sat in the front row, so it felt like my inevitable fate was taunting me slowly.

"I just want to get this over with," I was thinking when I heard, "Chi Chi," as most people called me because they couldn't call Chidinma without mispronouncing my name. I insist on them learning it now though.

"I am so, so sorry. For some reason, I couldn't find your paper." Ms. Cunningham continued, "I remember taking it from you during submission and taking it with the rest of the papers to my office, but I just can't find yours. I've searched everywhere. Can you please turn it in again?"

I couldn't believe my ears. I was stunned, shocked, speechless, all the words you can think of. Setting up the best poker face, I replied, "Oh, that's strange, okay, I'll turn it in first thing tomorrow morning." After my classes that day, I ran to my room, fell on my knees, and thanked God! I wrote a whole new paper and submitted it the next day.

I was in shock for days. I kept trying to understand

what had happened, but I couldn't. I was meant to be on my way out of school, but I had gotten an apology and a chance to resubmit instead. I wasn't the first or the last person to turn the assignment in, so it couldn't have been blown away by the air. Ms. Cunningham's office was two doors away from the classroom, so if it did get blown away, she would have seen it on the floor. I remembered her taking the assignments straight to her clean and highly organized office after class, so how did it go missing?

I was still asking so many questions when the Holy Spirit asked me, "You prayed for God's help, so why are you shocked that you got it?" This question humbled me. I quickly said, "God, I am so sorry for my unbelief. It's You again, it's always been You, and it'll always be You. Thank You!"

I couldn't stop thanking God. I always knew He answered prayers, but this was a different level of revelation for me. He actually sent an angel to take the paper out. Just when we think we have God figured out, He teaches us and makes us realize we really have no idea. He cannot be put in a box. There's nothing too small or too big for Him to do. God really loves to help us in every single way.

The unbelievable sounding miracles I had read of in the Bible stories had just happened to me. It still shocks me to this day. Not in disbelief anymore, but in the depth of the greatness and glory of God.

My father, my mother and I at my graduation

Chapter 5

GOD, MY HEALER

Growing up, I never had a problem making friends. I knew a lot of people and had a lot of people around me, but most of them knew little to nothing about me. They knew only what I wanted them to know and saw only what I wanted them to see. This was a result of the heartbreaking experiences I had endured from my childhood to my teenage years. I had "friends" who had lied on me, betrayed me, and didn't like me but liked the idea of being around me. This eventually made me very guarded and suspicious of everyone I met until proven otherwise.

As I got older, God healed my friendship circle and mended my heart with the best friends any girl could ask for, but it didn't stop my old habits from dying hard. I was a shoulder for my friends to lean on when they had problems, but I hardly divulged anything before they returned the favor towards me. To be fair, I had gotten so used to Jesus being my best friend, direct therapist, and problem solver that I didn't see the need to burden anyone with things they couldn't help me fix. The times I did divulge my problems,

I was looking to people for what I thought were the "little things" and looking to God for what I thought were the "big things."

In 2018, I was diagnosed with mild anemia. I focused on the "mild" before the anemia, so I put it in the "little things" category. I told my family and some friends, took my medicine as prescribed by the doctor, and casually kept moving. After a while, I started to wear the title as a badge of honor. I told whoever cared to listen, "Oh, I'm just tired because I have anemia," but I noticed that no matter how casual I tried to make it sound, I was suffering.

Getting out of bed became a difficult task. I felt weak 70 percent of the time. The inside of my eyelids and palms became very pale. Iron supplements became my best friends. At this point, the anemia definitely didn't seem so mild.

One day while visiting my parents in Port Harcourt, a thought came to me. "Chidinma, you haven't prayed about this anemia so you can get healed. Aren't you tired of it?" I usually talk to myself in third person when I'm having a serious conversation, so I thought it was just the voice in my head. I proceeded to join my family for dinner and decided I would pray about it later.

My sister Onyinye, who is also a pastor and prayer warrior, was visiting with her children that day, so I went into one of the rooms to spend some time with her before dinner. As I laid down next to her, she said, "Chidinma, I have a message for you. God said I should tell you that you haven't prayed to Him to heal the anemia. He said when you ask Him, He will heal you." I froze.

Once I regained some sort of consciousness, I went to my room and prayed. After praying, I thanked God for always thinking of me and I declared in faith that I was healed of anemia. As far as I was concerned, God said He would heal me once I prayed, so I was healed. Days went by, then weeks, then months, and there was no weakness or sickly feeling anymore. God healed me. I did my tests and there was no anemia in sight. God really healed me!

Before this encounter, it had never crossed my mind to pray for God's divine healing for the anemia because it was something I had medication to manage. It wasn't a life-or-death situation to me, so I saw it as something too small and worldly to bring to God. God was teaching me that just as there is nothing too big for Him to do, there is nothing too little for Him to do. He is concerned about every area of our lives. God's will is not for us to be sick; sin did that. By the death and resurrection power of Jesus, as born-again children in Christ, we are healed by Jesus' stripes. Through this healing, I also learned that as you get closer to God, the voice in your head stops being just your own but becomes that of the Holy Spirit in you, teaching you, growing you, and interceding for you.

> Ask, and it shall be given you; seek, and ye shall find; knock, and it shall be opened unto you. For every one that asketh receiveth; and he that seeketh. findeth; and to him that knocketh it shall be opened.

Matthew 7:7–8, KJV

This healing encounter taught me that God didn't want me to keep the little things for my friends alone but to bring them to Him as well. In true Chidinma fashion, I never stopped doing it.

Chapter 6

INTENTIONAL GOD

Look at the birds of the air, for they neither sow nor reap nor gather into barns; yet your heavenly Father feeds them. Are you not of more value than they?

Matthew 6:26, KJV

God is a good God. If it is not good, it is not God. In saying that, we have to be intentional in examining what "good" means to us because some things might be "good" from a human perspective, but God, who sees all, sees that it isn't good for us or good at all. In the same way, some things we think may be bad for us may actually work out for our good.

This is why we cannot lean on our own understanding. The human gauge of "goodness" is flawed. The flesh is self-serving and blinding. Only God is inherently Good. The Holy Spirit, who reveals all truth, is the only one who can guide us and convict us to know the truth of what is truly good and what is bad.

As Jesus started on his way, a man ran up to him and fell on his knees before him. "Good teacher," he asked, "what must I do to inherit eternal life?"

"Why do you call me good?" Jesus answered. "No one is good—except God alone."

Mark 10:17–18

There are three words I have learned on my journey so far: SURRENDER, OBEDIENCE, and TRUST.

Surrender all parts of your life—good and bad—to God.

Obey His directions as you worship Him in spirit and in truth. God is an authentic God; He doesn't like fakes. Obey Him, not out of fear, but out of love. Obedience to Him makes us live according to our true purpose and calling. It takes half of the unnecessary pain we put ourselves through in life away. God leads us in the right path to shield us from evil and save us from affliction.

Trust that God, who has brought you so far, will take you all the way. You can't be in a fruitful relationship with someone you don't trust. If we can trust human beings who are set to disappoint, why shouldn't we trust God, who is good, faithful, and void of lies in His nature? Trusting Him gives us peace and right direction in all things.

As we trust Him in life, we should also trust Him in times of death. Just because a loved one dies early doesn't mean God wasn't faithful in their life. Some people live long to see their purpose here on earth and some go earlier on to meet God in heaven. Either way, we should always be prepared because it is certain that we will all die, and no one knows when the hour shall come. It is better to live out eternity in heaven than to do life without God and live out eternity in hell.

> Precious in the sight of the Lord is the death of His saints.

Psalm 116:15

Once one of these is done, the rest comes easily. Obedience and Surrender come naturally when there is Trust. I think these are the three major keys to a great life with God.

When God asked me to break up with the man that I felt was the love of my life, I listened and I did. I wasn't sure what would happen next, but I knew God enough to know His track record. I trusted that He knew something I might not have known. As a Nigerian proverb says, "What an elder sees sitting down, a child would never be able to see if the child climbs the highest tree."

In my moment of sadness after making a phone call to end the relationship, God posed a question to me: "When I asked Abraham to sacrifice Isaac, did Isaac die?" Startled, I thought, "No, Isaac did not die." Even with that question, I made sure not to hope for anything or do anything other than what God had asked of me in the moment. I carried on in life with my new instruction to become single.

That man God asked me to break up with is my husband today. He is now the sweetest, most charming, and most intentional man. God used that time to work on parts of us that could not have been worked on while we were together. God was right. As good as he was, the former Josephus Jordan was not my husband, and the Chidinma Naze I was would not have been a good wife.

God broke us down to build us back up brick by brick. At the time, some may have seen this as torture, but I saw it as Love. Who God loves, He disciplines like the great Father He is. I saw that God loves us so much that He ordered our steps so we could have the best in each other for the sacrament of our marriage and life.

> My son, do not make light of the Lord's disci-
> pline, and do not lose heart when He rebukes
> you, because the Lord disciplines the one He

loves, and He chastens everyone He accepts as his son. Endure hardship as discipline; God is treating you as His children. For what children are not disciplined by their father? If you are not disciplined—and everyone undergoes discipline—then you are not legitimate, not true sons and daughters at all.

Moreover, we have all had human fathers who disciplined us and we respected them for it. How much more should we submit to the Father of spirits and live! They disciplined us for a little while as they thought best; but God disciplines us for our good, in order that we may share in His holiness. No discipline seems pleasant at the time, but painful. Later on, however, it produces a harvest of righteousness and peace for those who have been trained by it.

Hebrews 12:5–11

Chapter 7

GOD OF MIRACLES

My wedding was single-handedly one of the most amazing but highly stressful moments of my life. I had never seen something so beautiful cause so much anxiety and stress leading up to it. From the church requirements, the venue, the execution, to the steep prices. I confess, without any shame, that I cried more than once.

I really love anything with a view of water, so we chose to do a beach themed wedding at a beach in Lagos, Nigeria. My husband and I have friends and family around the world, so we picked a summer date in August to suit their schedules. Unknown to us, this was a blunder for those in Nigeria. Once people saw the date on the invitation cards, their follow-up comments were "August? It's rainy season, oh!" Some actually went on to declare matter-of-factly that it would rain at the wedding. Comment after comment, and my response was, "God won't let it rain at my wedding."

I was holding on to God's track record in my life and His recent lesson on His ability to do the little things for us.

Many times fear tried to creep in, but I rebuked it, saying, "God will not disappoint me," followed by "God, please, oh." Because at the end of the day, I am merely a pencil in the hand of my Creator. I wasn't trying to fight God if His will was for it to rain at the wedding.

I kept on praying with a side thought of, "What if it does rain at this wedding? What would I do then?" This subtle worry continued until I went to visit one of my aunties. While we were talking about the wedding, we had the usual August debate back and forth. We were at the "God will not disappoint me" part of the conversation when she said, "Okay, let's see how much God loves you." My heart skipped a beat and I quickly responded, "Ah! Now you have challenged my God! Thank you!"

I have learned from life experiences and from reading the Bible that God loves a good challenge. Telling God that He cannot do something pretty much seals the deal for that thing to be done (if it is His will). An example of this is what He did when the prophets of Baal doubted Elijah concerning God. He sent fire to consume the sacrifices and He sent rain over the land that had been in drought.

> After a long time, in the third year, the word of the LORD came to Elijah: "Go and present yourself to Ahab, and I will send rain on

the land." So Elijah went to present himself to Ahab.

1 Kings 18:1–2

The seventh time the servant reported, "A cloud as small as a man's hand is rising from the sea." So Elijah said, "Go and tell Ahab, 'Hitch up your chariot and go down before the rain stops you." Meanwhile, the sky grew black with clouds, the wind rose, a heavy rain started falling and Ahab rode off to Jezreel.

1 Kings 18:44–45

At the time for the evening sacrifice, the prophet Elijah went near the altar. "Lord, you are the God of Abraham, Isaac, and Israel," he prayed. "Prove that you are the God of Israel and that I am your servant. Show these people that you commanded me to do all these things. Lord, answer my prayer so these people will know that you, Lord, are God and that you will change their minds."

Then fire from the Lord came down and burned the sacrifice, the wood, the stones, and the ground around the altar. It also dried up the water in the ditch. When all the people saw this, they fell down to the ground, crying,

"The LORD is God! The LORD is God!"

1 Kings 18:36–39 (NCV)

During the wedding planning, my sister's friend, who is also a pastor, informed us that God told her to "tell Chidinma everything will be fine." I cried in gratitude to God after hearing that message. He knew I was going through a lot in that season and He wanted to comfort me like the good father He is. It made me even more confident that God was not going to let it rain and that everything was going to be fine. Jesus' first miracle was at the wedding in Canaan, so I trusted Him to do another at mine.

Two days to the wedding, it rained. A day to the wedding, it rained. On the day of the wedding, there was no rain! The only water in sight was the gorgeous blue water at the beach. The sky was clear and much sunnier than it had been all week. The view at the beach was spectacular. Once I saw it, I said a prayer of thanksgiving in my heart because I knew it was God. He made good on His word, as always.

I wasn't aware that those who worked at the beach were praying for me as well. When I arrived, they ran up to me saying, "It's not raining! We've all been praying for you since you booked this venue last year." They celebrated with me like they had seen all I had been through all those months. It made the moment even more precious.

In addition to the blessing of a sun-filled day, God performed many miracles between my husband and I that we would never forget. As God said it, He did it. Every single thing was fine. Even better than I could have planned or imagined. In Elijah's case, He sent rain. In mine, he halted it for a time, as only He has the power to do.

My husband and I at our traditional wedding

My husband and I at our beach reception after our church wedding

Chapter 8

GOD, MY SAVIOR

I think there's something beautiful about death. As painful as the loss can feel, it highlights the preciousness and volatility of life. For some, death is the end, but for others, it is the beginning.

As a Christian, it represents both. The end of our human lives here on earth, and the beginning of our lives either with God or the enemy of the soul. You get to spend eternity with whichever side you choose, the light or the darkness, because God honors free will.

Whether death represents an end or beginning for you, one thing is certain—it will come and it is finite, but those who live in Christ Jesus never die.

> Jesus said to her, 'I am the resurrection and the life. The one who believes in me will live, even though they die; and whoever lives by believing in me will never die'.

John 11:25–26

For I take no pleasure in the death of anyone,
declares the Sovereign Lord. Repent and live!.

Ezekiel 18:32

I started out these stories of God's miracles in my life by talking about a near-death experience in my childhood, so trust God's sense of humor and strategic planning to have me end it with another near-death experience in my adulthood. As gory as that sounds, I am the vessel of the Lord Most High, so I move as I am led.

Two months after moving to Nigeria in 2016, I became riddled with severe pains on the lower right side of my abdomen. I went to the hospital, and after some tests, I was told I had an appendix that needed to be surgically removed immediately.

I had undergone many other surgeries prior to this due to other health issues, but this surgery scared me like never before. The pain of the appendix was excruciating, and in a very unusual manner for me, my spirit didn't feel at peace. I was usually the girl who would make jokes with the doctors and nurses while being wheeled to the operating room, but that didn't happen this time. On the day of my surgery, I felt uncomfortable.

While being moved to the operating room, I began to

pray silently. My mum had prayed for me earlier, but I felt the need to have my one-on-one time with God. As the surgery was about to begin, an anesthesiologist came in, administered the anesthesia, and left. As the surgeon cut me open, I noticed that I could feel something unusual. It began as the feeling of a slight tug on my skin but quickly progressed to very sharp pains. I realized that I could feel every incision the surgeon was making. This confused me and put me in a bigger state of panic because I knew that the whole point of the anesthesia was to numb the area.

I became very uncomfortable in a way I had never experienced, and I started to scream and call out at the top of my voice, "Jesus! Jesus! Jesus! Please help me!" I was very afraid. Writing it or explaining it could never fully describe what I was going through.

Once the doctors saw what was happening, they injected me with something that made me become unconscious. To them I had knocked out, but instead, I was getting pulled into a winding multicolored portal, like the ones we see in movies. The portal continued for what seemed like many minutes, when suddenly I was thrust into a place filled with many clouds. It looked like I was in the sky, but I could sense it wasn't the sky. This place was filled with people who looked, as I said while explaining to my sister Chinonso, "really white." She helped me realize they weren't white, but they were light. As I went back to the moment, I realized she was right. Their faces were full of light. Very bright lights.

As I was standing there, I noticed someone standing to the left of me. I turned to look and, to my surprise, it was Jesus. Immediately, I no longer felt fear. I felt total peace. I felt at home like I was in a place I had been before. I did not think of anything. Not my family, not my friends, not the world, nothing. The only place that existed in my mind was exactly where I was standing. I felt comfortable right next to Him.

As He looked at me, I could tell He wasn't very happy with me.

Before I could process that, He led me to a corner where children were sitting cross-legged on the floor and directed me to teach them. I proceeded to teach the children without asking any questions. Everything I needed to do just came to me naturally. I taught the children for a while before Jesus came back. I noticed He never left me. Sometimes He was by my side and other times He was watching me from a close distance. He held my hand, signaling that it was time for me to return, and again, I was thrown into another winding portal.

The portal seemed longer than the first one, but this time I woke up to the sound of voices—my brother Ekeneme's voice, my mother's voice, and the nurse's voice. I could hear everyone and all they said, but I could not open my eyes and I could not move my body. It felt like I was trapped in my body and no one knew I was there. I tried to scream out to them, but I couldn't.

This continued for minutes until suddenly, I felt my brother rubbing my right hand. As he rubbed my hands, I began coming back fully to life. It felt like I needed to keep feeling his touch to bring me back to this side. I kept hoping and praying he didn't stop. Thankfully, he never did. As he continued, I opened my eyes.

I want to clarify that the events of this surgery do not mean that I had bad or inexperienced doctors. In fact, my doctors were great. The weight of the events at the hospital do not rest on them but on the journey God was taking me through. There were complications during the surgery that I have not been led by God to share yet. All that occurred was more spiritual than physical. If not for the grace of God, I could have died that day.

I know many people do not believe in the spiritual aspects of life, but I have experienced enough to know that we are spiritual beings living a human existence for a designated time. As God says, the flesh is weak but the spirit is willing.

I mentioned earlier that Jesus didn't look very happy with me when I saw Him. Before that encounter, I had been living in sin. I wasn't born again. To be honest, even after that encounter, it took me a while to fully let go and let the Holy Spirit help me fully commit my life to God. As a child raised in a Christian home, I always knew God. In my personal journey away from my family, I always felt the presence of God and prayed to Him, but a lot of times I was putting my empty desires and the things of the world before God.

In my mind, I thought I loved God, but my definition of Love wasn't God's definition of love. Back then my definition of love was just a feeling. It was me doing whatever I wanted for my own pleasure, even when it displeased God and others.

God has taught me, just as Jesus said in the Bible, that if you love Him you will keep His commandments (John 14:15). So when we don't keep God's commandments, especially when we are aware of them, we are not loving or serving Him in spirit and in truth.

Whenever I reflect on my past and the culture of sin, I

think how ungrateful we humans can be. God created us, gave us life, forgives us over and over again, but we still sin against Him because of our selfish desires that only lead to death. It makes me think if we can hurt so deeply when people betray us, how does God, our Creator, feel when we betray him? On the other hand, it teaches me that if God can put all that aside and forgive us when we come to Him, I should also always forgive others.

To put this in perspective, my encounter with Jesus during the surgery was in 2016, but I didn't begin my born-again journey until 2020. I call it a journey because even with all God has taught me, I still need God's help and there is still so much to learn. As human beings, we are not perfect, but making a decision to keep getting up no matter how many times we fall keeps us on the path with God. Born again doesn't mean living in ultimate perfection. Born again simply means letting go of the lies of the enemy and surrendering totally to the Holy Spirit, who makes all things new. People who are born again fail too, but when the Holy Spirit teaches you, you'll realize that you should never believe the lie of the enemy that your shame outweighs the grace of God.

You should not intentionally fall just because there is grace—that becomes deception—but you should know that in getting back up, asking for God's forgiveness and doing better, you are letting God know that you, too, would never give up on Him.

Fully committing to God was something I had prayed many times about because I knew I couldn't do it without His help. No matter how many times I fell, I got back up and prayed for God's help again. In my free will, I chose Him, but moving forward I had to choose Him with my actions, thoughts, words, and everything I was.

On the first day of lent 2020, the priest, while blessing the ashes, said, "After this lent, you will not be the same." I knew immediately that he was talking to me. I claimed it with a resounding, "Amen." After that, it was one big refining moment after another between God and me. It was not an easy journey, but with the pain of shedding parts of myself came an unexplainable joy. With the help of the Holy Spirit, things that once seemed difficult to let go of became much easier. My eyes began to open in a different way. My ears began to truly hear and understand. I learned that when the bible said we should run away from evil things, it meant run and not catwalk or stroll alongside.

For many years I had struggled, but now I am on a refining journey. I don't know how much more refining I have on the journey, but I am thankful because only those who are dead are truly done. I am still alive, and I am thankful that God, in His infinite mercy, did not give up on me. I could have died in the shame of my past, but thankfully, before God formed me, He knew me and He made plans for me. God saved me. The Bible says that the wages of sin is death, so God didn't just save me from physical death, He saved me from spiritual death.

When I woke up from surgery, I asked my brother why he was rubbing my hands the way he was and at the time he was. He casually responded, "I don't know. I just felt like I needed to touch you in that way, so I did." I had never been so thankful for a hand rub in my life.

I used to wonder what would have happened to me if my brother wasn't at the hospital at that time or didn't touch me when he felt the need. One day while pondering on it, God responded to me that the same God who had a donkey waiting for the disciples and had a ram available for Abraham to sacrifice in place of his son Isaac, always makes provisions. Hallelujah!

> As he approached Bethphage and Bethany at the hill called the Mount of Olives, he sent two of his disciples, saying to them, "Go to the village ahead of you, and as you enter it, you will find a colt tied there, which no one has ever ridden. Untie it and bring it here. If anyone asks you, 'Why are you

untying it?' say, 'The Lord needs it.'

Luke 19:29–31

"Do not lay a hand on the boy," he said. "Do not do anything to him. Now I know that you fear God, because you have not withheld from me your son, your only son." Abraham looked up and there in a thicket he saw a ram caught by its horns. He went over and took the ram and sacrificed it as a burnt offering instead of his son. So Abraham called that place The LORD Will Provide.

Genesis 22:12–14

I wrote earlier that God was ending this story with a near-death experience. I thought He had a sense of humor then, but as He is leading me to write about another miracle that has recently unfolded, I see yet again that He is truly good. The final story in this book isn't one of death, but instead, one of New Life, just as the book started.

Chapter 9

GOD, MY MOUTHPIECE

I had always been taught in church that God knows our most inner thoughts. He sees the yearnings of our hearts and the words we never speak out loud, so He knows who we truly are, not just who the world thinks we are. As Proverbs 23 says, "As a man thinketh in his heart, so is he."

I had always known I wanted to have children. Even when I didn't think I wanted to get married, I knew I wanted children. As a child, I loved children so much that I thought I would become a pediatrician. That dream quickly died when I realized that to be a doctor, I needed to be friendly with my high school foes, science and math, so I switched to the dream of becoming a news person like Oprah instead.

As I grew older, I shared my feelings of having children with my boyfriend at the time, who is now my husband, Josephus. We had always been big on communicating our feelings, so we had these conversations easily and frequently. As we kept having these conversations, I noticed that something felt different. I started to ask him questions like, "What would you do if you found out I couldn't have children?" At first I thought it was just me throwing out questions to test his mindset on certain issues or how he would handle scenarios beyond his control, but in time I realized it was more. I had this indescribable fear and worry in my heart that I might have some difficulty having children. This filled my mind with worry because I had never been one to plan for my future, but having my own children was one thing I had always planned towards.

With no basis for my feelings of worry, all I did was ask my boyfriend more questions. He caught on to the pattern, so instead of answering the questions, he reassured me that we were fine and would have as many children as we please.

This feeling persisted from 2013 to 2016, from some of my time in college, to the time I had moved back to Nigeria.

In 2016, some months after the appendix surgery and my move from Port Harcourt to Lagos, my sister Onyinye called me on the phone. While talking and catching up in our usual fashion, she said, "Chidinma, I called to give you a message from God today." I was excited because at this point I had become aware that God also spoke to me through her.

She continued, "After you had your surgery, God told me to sow a seed of offering for you in church. I did and forgot about it until now. Today, He showed me when you were worrying about having children and the things you asked Joe about children. He said I should tell you that the seed He instructed me to sow has been fruitful and you should no longer worry because you won't experience any difficulties having children."

I had never shared these concerns with anyone other than my boyfriend, Joe, and Joe did not share it with anyone. At the time, he and my sister had not even met because I was strict about not introducing any boyfriend to my family until I had agreed to be a wife. There was no way my sister could have known about this on her own.

As my sister explained further, I realized that my worry was a sign of something that could have actually occurred. God usually talks to me or prompts me to pray through my feelings; but this time, I didn't feel the need to pray. I just worried, complained, and forgot about it. I noticed that I had stopped feeling worried some months before my sister's call, but I just thought it was my busy schedule that clouded my mind with other things. It wasn't until that moment that I realized I was no longer worrying because

God had taken care of the situation.

Once I got off the phone with my sister, I wailed. I couldn't speak for a long time after crying. All I could think of was how God went ahead of me to sort out an issue I didn't even understand and had never talked to Him or anyone about other than Joe.

God doesn't need man to be the God He is; He is God all by Himself.

On April 2, 2023, before heading to Palm Sunday mass, Josephus and I found out that I was pregnant. On December 4, 2024, our son, Josephus Tobechukwu Jordan Jr. was born.

> When the LORD brought back the captives to Zion, we were like men who dreamed. Our mouths were filled with laughter, our tongues with songs of joy. Then it was said among the nations, 'The LORD has done great things for them'.

> **Psalm 126:1, NKJV**

Chapter 10

GOD, THE NAME CHANGER

But now, thus says the LORD, who created you, Jacob, and formed you, Israel: Do not fear, for I have redeemed you; I have called you by name: you are mine.

Isaiah 43:1, NABRE

When God calls you by a name, that is the name that defines your life. The sins you commit could make you see yourself as less and make you believe the negative titles the world/the devil tries to give you—I know at some point I did—but as the song goes, "Amazing grace, how sweet the sound that saved a wretch like me. I once was lost but now I'm found, was blind but now I see."

There were many times I was deep in sin, but everyone who laid their hands on my head to pray would call me "the apple of God's eye" or "Daughter of Zion." In my mind, I would ask God, "How? Do these people even know what they are talking about?"

I thought they were mistaken because they couldn't see my secrets, but all along it was me who was blind. Blind and vision blurred by sin. Buried in shame and mistaking that shame for self-reflection.

In the Igbo culture, we say that a person's name follows him/her. I used to say that a name is like a tribal mark you can't wipe off. No matter how far someone runs or how many times they change their name on paper, they could never escape who they really are. I've come to realize that I was partially wrong. Names are powerful because as people call upon you, they profess the meaning of that name, but it is not always as permanent as a tribal mark. God can give and change the name and behavior of anyone He sees fit, especially if the person is willing. Many times in the Bible, He changed people's names and elevated their characters and positions. Abram became Abraham; Jacob became Israel; Saul had one of the most drastic changes and became Paul. We never know who we are until God tells us. Only the Creator can truly inform the creation.

In my case, God had always been trying to tell me who I am from the beginning. My grandfather used to call me Chikaodinaka, which means "it is in God's hands." Fast forward to many years after his death, God instructed me to say the prayer, "Carry me in your hands, Jesus, so I don't hit my feet against a stone."

After the incident at my birth, my mother called me CHIDINMA—God Is Good, because God, who is always good, saved our lives. He has surely shown Himself Good in my life. As a pastor called Bidemi Mark Mordi once said, "A name is a prophecy in motion."[1]

No matter the sins we have committed, God's love for us does not change and His grace is sufficient at all times. "Nothing can separate us from the love of God" (Romans 8:39). He only intends that we catch up to who He truly calls us to be and not the label sin puts on us. He intends we get up out of the enemy's lies, deceit, and shame to walk confidently into the name He, our God, has given us. That way, we can manifest as His children in the land of the living, and His will for us will be done on earth as it is in heaven.

> Yet to all who did receive him, to those who believed in his name, he gave the right to become children of God.

> **John 1:12**

> Obey the LORD your God and keep his commands and decrees that are written in this Book

of the Law and turn to the Lᴏʀᴅ your God with all your heart and with all your soul.

Now what I am commanding you today is not too difficult for you or beyond your reach. It is not up in heaven, so that you have to ask, "Who will ascend into heaven to get it and proclaim it to us so we may obey it?" Nor is it beyond the sea, so that you have to ask, "Who will cross the sea to get it and proclaim it to us so we may obey it?" No, the word is very near you; it is in your mouth and in your heart so you may obey it.

Deuteronomy 30:10–14

Epilogue

When having conversations about heaven, hell, and the consequences of sin, some people often ask, "Aren't we all children of God? If we are all saved by grace, doesn't that mean we don't need to do anything else to go to heaven?" My response is, yes, we all are, but if you deny your father, move away from him, and never contact him, do you get all the perks that come with being in his presence and having a relationship with him? When you don't call him, do you still hear his voice? Do you know what's happening in his life? Do you know the plans he has for you and the gifts he has in store? Would you be certain that you would be a beneficiary in his will if he had one? (We are called co-heirs with Christ after all, Romans 8:17.) I believe that's how our relationship with God is. It is not just a one-sided relationship where we take, take, and take again. If that were the case, God wouldn't have given Adam and Eve the option to decide whether or not to obey Him and not eat from the tree of the knowledge of good and evil. He could have hidden the tree from them or not created it at all, but He wanted them to choose to do the right thing. He wanted them to choose Him in love, just as He wants us to choose Him now.

Typically, parents have the power to disown children, but in God's case, He has chosen us and free will has given us, the children, the power to choose also. The farther you distance yourself from God, the more you disown Him and cut Him off from your life. Thankfully, God is not exactly like our human parents. He is rich in mercy, kindness, compassion, and freely gives this thing called "grace," which gives us the option to return and access to Him whenever we do.

We are always meant to be keyed in to learn and grow in God in every time and season. To hear from Him, to be taught by Him, and to be guided by His Holy Spirit. Naturally, children are not meant to walk alone or else they could get lost.

> Remain in me, as I also remain in you. No branch can bear fruit by itself; it must remain in the vine. Neither can you bear fruit unless you remain in me. I am the vine; you are the branches. If you remain in me and I in you, you will bear much fruit; apart from me you can do nothing. If you do not remain in me, you are like a branch that is thrown away and withers; such branches are picked up, thrown into the fire and burned.

John 15: 4–6

I have learned that God's grace is sufficient, but like a birthday gift dropped off on your doorstep, you have to go open the door and pick it up. You have to be ready to receive the gift. This is the one gift you don't have to beg for to receive. This is the one item you don't have to post on your social media as a hint for your friends. It is already available to you since your birth. It is sufficient for everyone.

Let us remember that God's grace, being sufficient, does not give us the pass to live immoral lives. It is available to ensure we have continued access to return to our father regardless of the numerous times we err. It is a gift of love from God our Creator that is not to be tarnished or taken for granted.

> Praise be to the God and Father of our Lord Jesus Christ, who has blessed us in the heavenly realms with every spiritual blessing in Christ. For he chose us in him before the creation of the world to be holy and blameless in his sight. In love He predestined us for adoption to sonship through Jesus Christ, in accordance with his pleasure and will to the praise of his glorious grace, which he has freely given us in the One he loves. In him we have redemption through his blood, the forgiveness of sins, in accordance

with the riches of God's grace that he lavished
on us.

Ephesians 1: 3–8

For it is by grace you have been saved, through
faith—and this is not from yourselves, it is the
gift of God—not by works, so that no one can
boast. For we are God's handiwork, created in
Christ Jesus to do good works, which God prepared in advance for us to do.

Ephesians 2: 8–10

Afterword

While writing this, I asked myself the question that had haunted me for many years due to my past life experiences. "Chidinma, what if people read this and think you're bragging?" Yes, I talk about the difficulties I've experienced in life, but they all end well.

As I thought about this I realized rhetorically, "Isn't that the product of being in Christ Jesus?" Through the inspiration of God, David promised us in Psalm 23 that "surely God's goodness and mercy shall follow us all the days of our lives." Not some days of our lives, not only good days of our lives, even when we don't feel it; God's goodness and mercy are with us abundantly ALL the days of our lives.

As I get more intimate with God, I've realized that life is not hard with Jesus. He teaches us some lessons that could feel daunting and difficult, but even those are for us to graduate to better places. Everything He does is really for our good and ultimately for our joy because according to Jeremiah 29:11, His plans are to prosper us and to give us an expected end. Not always as we expect by our human understanding, but as He expects for His will to be done on earth and in our lives as it is in heaven. When we understand this through the revelation of the Holy Spirit, we understand life and ultimately, live in ease and the peace of God that surpasses all understanding.

Proverbs 13:15 says, "Good understanding gives favor but the way of the transgressor is hard." To transgress means to go against a law, rule, code, or conduct. Only when we go against the rule of God and the code in which He has set for us to operate, do we really have it hard.

We all have an innate need to serve that which is greater than us, and that is God, our Creator. People who don't, usually feel an emptiness within. They often feel lost and end up idolizing things such as money, clothes, cars, the sun, moon, or "the universe" to fill the void.

No matter your transgressions, God is there, waiting for you with open arms. I encourage you to open up to His Holy Spirit today. Bad things may have happened to you, but it doesn't negate who God is and His ability to save you. Let go of it all and let God take control as only Him can. Form a relationship with God and love Him for who He is and not out of fear. God's word is truth and life. He is waiting for you with open arms. I pray you run into Him today.

Every person's story isn't the same, but that doesn't

mean one person is more blessed than the other. Instead, it shows that we are all uniquely made and have different needs and beauty in our peculiarities. We are all children of God and we all have our own purpose, paths, and most importantly, our own names given to glorify God, our Creator.

This book is a compilation of things I have been through, but it is not just about me. It is about God and how He helped me overcome every pain, sickness, and turmoil. I pray you let Him do what needs to be done in your life.

As my lovely earthly father, Mr. Fidelis Naze, always sings,

> Great is Thy faithfulness
> Great is Thy faithfulness
> Morning by morning new mercies I see
> All I have needed God's hands have provided
> Great is Thy faithfulness, Lord unto me.

I hope this blesses you, gives you hope, and reminds you of the limitless and incredible love of God. His Greatness, His Kindness, His Intentionality, His Faithfulness, His Mercy, and His Love are second to none. I give Him all the Glory!

I am here to testify that God is real, God is true, and CHIDINMA—GOD IS GOOD.

CHÍDÌNMÁ: GOD IS GOOD

O Lord, you have examined my heart
and know everything about me.
You know when I sit down or stand up.
You know my thoughts even when I'm far away.
You see me when I travel
and when I rest at home.
You know everything I do.
You know what I am going to say
even before I say it, Lord.
You go before me and follow me.
You place your hand of blessing on my head.
Such knowledge is too wonderful for me,
too great for me to understand!

I can never escape from your Spirit!
I can never get away from your presence!
If I go up to heaven, you are there;
if I go down to the grave, you are there.
If I ride the wings of the morning,
if I dwell by the farthest oceans,
even there your hand will guide me,
and your strength will support me.
I could ask the darkness to hide me
and the light around me to become night—
but even in darkness I cannot hide from you.
To you the night shines as bright as day.

Darkness and light are the same to you.

You made all the delicate, inner parts of my body
and knit me together in my mother's womb.
Thank you for making me so wonderfully complex!
Your workmanship is marvelous—how well I know it.
You watched me as I was being formed in utter seclusion,
as I was woven together in the dark of the womb.
You saw me before I was born.
Every day of my life was recorded in your book.
Every moment was laid out
before a single day had passed.

How precious are your thoughts about me, O God.
They cannot be numbered!
I can't even count them;
they outnumber the grains of sand!
And when I wake up,
you are still with me!

Search me, O God, and know my heart;
test me and know my anxious thoughts.
Point out anything in me that offends you,
and lead me along the path of everlasting life.

Psalm 139 (NLT)

Gratitude Check

"And the LORD **answered me:** 'Write the vision; make it plain on tablets, so he may run who reads it'" (**Habakkuk 2:2, ESV**).

Before you begin, please go to a quiet place, sit in stillness with God and let Him guide you through this journey. Walk with Him as He guides you through.

What are you grateful for today?

I _____ (your name)
am grateful for _____

_____

_____

_____

_____

_____

What aren't you grateful for today? _____

_____

_____

_____

_____

_____

_____

How does your worry impact your situation? Positively/ Negatively (circle one).

Now, pray against any situation in your life that is trying to keep you in a place of fear and worry.

- Invite God to take control of it

- Ask the Holy Spirit to fill you, renew your heart, and help you never believe the lies of the enemy over the voice of God.

  Create in me a clean heart, oh God; and renew a right spirit within me.

  Psalm 51:10 KJV

  We demolish arguments and every preten-sion that sets itself up against the knowledge of God, and we take captive every thought to make it obedient to Christ.

  2 Corinthians 10:5

- Now, praise and worship God your Creator and Savior. Put the devil and his evil works to shame.

- Testify to all that God has made you to be and ask the Holy Spirit to reveal more to you.

- The word of God is a double-edged sword that cuts

through every place and situation. Speak the word of God over your life.

You are the salt of the earth.

Matthew 5:13

You are the light of the world. A town built on a hill cannot be hidden.

Matthew 5:14

I can do all things through Christ who strengthens me.

Philippians 4:13 (NKJV)

But He was wounded for our transgressions, He was bruised for our iniquities; The chastisement for our peace was upon Him, and by His stripes we are healed.

Isaiah 53:5 (NKJV)

And they overcame him by the blood of the Lamb, and by the word of their testimony; and they loved not their lives unto the death.

Revelation 12:11 (KJV)

For I know the plans I have for you," declares the LORD, "plans to prosper you and not to harm you, plans to give you hope and a future.

Jeremiah 29:11

The Lord is my shepherd; I shall not want.

Psalm 23 (KJV)

Whoever dwells in the shelter of the Most High will rest in the shadow of the Almighty. I will say of the LORD, "He is my refuge and my fortress, my God, in whom I trust...

Psalm 91

Give thanks to the LORD, for he is good;
his love endures forever.

Let Israel say:
"His love endures forever."
Let the house of Aaron say:
"His love endures forever."
Let those who fear the LORD **say:**
"His love endures forever."

When hard pressed, I cried to the LORD;
he brought me into a spacious place.
The LORD **is with me; I will not be afraid.**

What can mere mortals do to me?
The LORD **is with me; he is my helper.**
I look in triumph on my enemies.

It is better to take refuge in the LORD
than to trust in humans.
It is better to take refuge in the LORD
than to trust in princes.
All the nations surrounded me,
but in the name of the LORD **I cut them down.**
They surrounded me on every side,
but in the name of the LORD **I cut them down.**
They swarmed around me like bees,
but they were consumed as quickly as burning thorns;
in the name of the LORD **I cut them down.**
I was pushed back and about to fall,
but the LORD **helped me.**
The LORD **is my strength and my defense;**
he has become my salvation.

Shouts of joy and victory
resound in the tents of the righteous:
"The LORD's right hand has done mighty things!
The LORD's right hand is lifted high;
the LORD's right hand has done mighty things!"
I will not die but live,
and will proclaim what the LORD **has done.**
The LORD **has chastened me severely,**
but he has not given me over to death.

Open for me the gates of the righteous;
I will enter and give thanks to the LORD.
This is the gate of the LORD
through which the righteous may enter.
I will give you thanks, for you answered me;
you have become my salvation.

The stone the builders rejected
has become the cornerstone;
the LORD **has done this,**
and it is marvelous in our eyes.
The LORD **has done it this very day;**
let us rejoice today and be glad.

LORD, save us!
LORD, grant us success!

Blessed is he who comes in the name of the LORD.
From the house of the LORD **we bless you.**
The LORD **is God,**
and he has made his light shine on us.
With boughs in hand, join in the festal procession
up to the horns of the altar.

You are my God, and I will praise you;
you are my God, and I will exalt you.

Give thanks to the LORD, for he is good;
his love endures forever.

Psalm 118

Praise the LORD, all you servants of the LORD
who minister by night in the house of the LORD.
Lift up your hands in the sanctuary and praise
the LORD. May the Lord bless you from Zion,
he who is the Maker of heaven and earth.

Psalm 134

Thank God for the gift of faith and ask Him to bless
you with more faith in all circumstances.

"Count your blessings, name them one by one, and it
will surprise you what the Lord has done."

Look at the birds of the air; they do not sow or
reap or store away in barns, and yet your heavenly Father feeds them. Are you not much more
valuable than they? Can any one of you by worrying add a single hour to your life?

Matthew 6:26–27, NIV

Now remember that you are a new creature in Christ
Jesus and by the stripes of Jesus you are healed.

- Write again, but this time, write the wonderful
  things God has done for you throughout the years.

- Reflect on them and remember that He who has
  brought you this far is surely too faithful to fail or
  desert you.

Let us then approach God's throne of grace
with confidence, so that we may receive mercy
and find grace to help us in our time of need.

Hebrews 4:16

Though my father and mother forsake me, the
Lord will receive me.

Psalm 27:10

For the Lord loves the just and will not forsake
His faithful ones.

Psalm 37:28

The Lord is your keeper; the Lord is your shade
on your right hand.

Psalm 121:5 (ESV)

I will instruct you and teach you in the way you
should go; I will counsel you with my eye upon
you.

Psalm 32:8 (ESV)

Be strong and courageous. Do not be afraid or
terrified because of them, for the LORD your
God goes with you; he will never leave you nor
forsake you.

Deuteronomy 31:6–8

And if the Spirit of Him who raised Jesus from
the dead is living in you, He who raised Christ
from the dead will also give life to your mortal
bodies because of His Spirit who lives in you.

Romans 8:11

I say to myself, "The Lord is my portion; there-
fore, I will wait for Him.

Lamentation 3:24

My son, do not forget my teaching, but keep
my commands in your heart, for they will pro-
long your life many years and bring you peace
and prosperity. Let love and faithfulness never
leave you; bind them around your neck, write
them on the tablet of your heart. Then you will
win favor and a good name in the sight of God
and man. Trust in the LORD with all your heart
and lean not on your own understanding; in
all your ways submit to him, and he will make
your paths straight. Do not be wise in your own
eyes; fear the LORD and shun evil. This will
bring health to your body and nourishment to
your bones. Honor the LORD with your wealth,
with the first fruits of all your crops; then your
barns will be filled to overflowing, and your
vats will brim over with new wine.

Proverbs 3:1–10

The Lord bless you and keep you; the Lord make his face shine on you and be gracious to you; the Lord turn his face toward you and give you peace.

Numbers 6:24–26

Glossary

Mammy Market — A market attached to a barrack where products for soldiers and Youth Corpers are sold. Mainly in Nigeria.

NEPA now PHCN (Power Holding Company of Nigeria) — This power bill is usually exorbitant.

"Oh" — One of the many ways Nigerians exclaim.

Pidgin English — Nigerian pidgin is an English based creole language spoken as a lingua franca across Nigeria. It is also referred to as Broken English.

PPA Letter — Place of Primary Assignment. This letter contains the service location assigned to a Nigerian National Youth Corper.

"You don get am" — You have gotten it.

"Yes oh I don get am" — Yes I agree; I have gotten it.

About the Author

Chidinma Naze is a child of God, wife, and mother. Born as the sixth child to two God-loving parents, Chidinma has always loved God and community. Chidinma graduated from the University of Indianapolis with a degree in communication. She has worked as a digital media strategist for over seven years and has contributed to the success of several movies, TV shows, and brands. Chidinma's ability to listen to and trust in the will of God is the driving force behind her decisions. Her goal for this book is to share the good works of the Lord and to help others build unwavering faith and know that Jesus is real and God is good.

Endnotes

1   Mark-Mordi, Bidemi. 2023. Instagram. October 9, 2023. https://www.instagram.com/reel/CyKtYtStas3/.

9 798893 333374